Sirius

Sirius

TOM CINTULA

Copyright © 2022 by Tom Cintula.

Library of Congress Control Number:	2022912399
ISBN:	Hardcover	978-1-6698-3634-6
	Softcover	978-1-6698-3633-9
	eBook	978-1-6698-3534-9

All rights reserved. No part of this book may be reproduced or transmitted in any form or by any means, electronic or mechanical, including photocopying, recording, or by any information storage and retrieval system, without permission in writing from the copyright owner.

Any people depicted in stock imagery provided by Getty Images are models, and such images are being used for illustrative purposes only.
Certain stock imagery © Getty Images.

Print information available on the last page.

Rev. date: 08/30/2022

To order additional copies of this book, contact:
Xlibris
844-714-8691
www.Xlibris.com
Orders@Xlibris.com
844287

CONTENTS

EXPERIMENTAL POEMS

Excitement 1
Freight Train 2
Heavy Metal 3
Sunset on The Beach 4
Embedded Spirits 5
Oblivious World 6
Hardcore 7
On The Brink of Disaster 8
Spent 9
Insomnia 10
Another Overnight Shift at CVS 11
Good vs. Evil 12
The New Breed 13
Underground Shock Rocker 14
A Poem About Worklike Bullshit 15
To Live 16
Fawned By A Crush 17

VILLANELLE POEMS

I Can't Say "No". 21
Rockin' The Leather 22
Dark Clouds, Heavy Winds, And Tears Of Sorrow 23
The Peacemaker 24
Sanity Is Bad For The Spirit 25
To Kiss Or Kill 26

The Real Devil	27
The Shock	28
Love Is A Mental Health Issue For All	29
It's Never "I", It's Always "We"	30
The Frozen Pond	31
The Mountains	32
No Security In The World	33
Crying Is A Room Of Piercing Eyeballs	34
Heavy Hearts	35
My Fear Follows Me	36
That Thundering Feeling	37
A Drag to Smile	38
Wanna Lose My Mind	39
Sometimes The World's Not Ready For You	40
Exhausted Alone	41
There Are Day Where I feel Like Killing You	42
Strong While Weak	43
That Shit Hurt	44
Owen 3:16 says "I Just Broke Your Neck."	45
Love And Lust Intertwine	46
Just One Chance at Love	47
Heavy Eyes	48
Everything Is Fake	49
A Still Beating Heart	50
Supermodel Satan	51
Dance Of Combat	52
Sore And Tired	53
Comatose by Hypnotism	54
My Heart Is A Jigsaw Puzzle	55
Roar With Reason	56
Fall To Rise	57
To Surf Is To Climb	58
I Will Fuck You In The Face With My Fist	59
Blood Out Of A Rock	60
More Harm Than We Need	61

Blacklisted By A Prostitute	62
I Feel That Nobody Likes Me	63
The Metaphysics Of Bad Luck	64
Roar For Serenity	65
Frailty Of The Heart	66
Facing Life Alone	67
The Sun Is Watching	68
Soul From Mind	69
A Battered Soul Is A Stronger Mind	70
Chained To A Bomb With No Shallow End	71
Have Mood, Will Travel	72
The Potholes To Adventure	73
The Melt Of Romance	74
The Dread of Existential Choice	75
Strong Emotions Wear You Out	76
The Only Way Out: Suicide	77
Big-Time Bomb	78
Lookin' Out For #1	79
Life Is A Clutter	80
Miracle Of Strength	81
Journeyman's Road	82
L-O-V-E	83
Splosh My Bones	84
Wanderin' 'Round The World	85
Clueless	86
Invisible Forces	87
A Heart Of Gold Is A Spirit Of Pain	88

SONNET POEMS

What Is Paradise Exactly?	91
Weak From Head To Toe	92
To Sleep Only To Never Wake	93
Love: Good For The Soul, Bad For The Mind	94
Chapels Of The Bleak	95

The Difference Between Good And Evil	96
Lovelorn, But Not Loved	97
Answering To the Herd	98
Flowers	99
A Mind That Segues At Warp Speed	100
Pay To Play	101
Black Hole of Pop Culture	102
Junk Food Are Drugs	103
Unchained	104
Body at Ease	105
Burning Hearts	106
Venom in Our Veins	107
Shames and Flukes	108
Disheartenment and Enchantment	109
Battlefield Of Hate	110
Marathon Of Doom	111
Living Our Raw Thoughts	112
Blinded By The Arctic	113
Waking Up Is Hard To Do	114
Strike Like A Ram Without A Damn	115
Whirlwind of Raw Emotion	116
Never Rest in Peace	117
To Control Is to Protect	118
Life	119
Arnie Pye In The Sky	120
Two-Faced Behemoth	121
Point of No Return	122
Chasing a Living	123
The Neighborhood	124
I Can't Sleep Because I Won't Sleep	125
Big Game Hunting	126

FREE VERSE POEMS

Where's Sam?	129
Bitterness	130
A Broken Heart Always Beats	131
Weather Is a Mood	132
Uncertainty Is a Certainty	133
Lights Out	134
Where's the Love?	135
Experience the Heat	136
Soulful World	137
Who Am I?	138
The Mystery Of Life	139
The Author of Repressed Rage	140
The Illusion of Happiness	142
Gold: Color of Champions	143
Steam of Failures	145
The Chore of Trust	147
Force	149
Spirit of Metal	151
Clinging Onto Love	153
The Farther Away, The More Beautiful	154
Pain Is Strength	155
Just Not In The Cards	156
Anger is Suicide For All Of Us	157
Shit Is an Omniscient Chameleon	158
Money Is The #1 Problem For Us All	159
The Inner Turmoil Showcase	160
The Main Event	162

Tom Cintula is an independent author and writer who was born, raised and currently resides in Staten Island, New York. He is a graduate of The College of Staten Island with a bachelor's degree in Sociology and Anthropology. His previous publishing effort includes the debut poetry collection, Sonnetsphere. His previous writing credits include contributions for The Borgen Project, Tribune Sports, and All Access MMA.

As the brightest star in the night sky, we all look to shine above the darkness. As Sirius is the glowing light among the rest of the stars, we all imagine ourselves as that star, where there are other stars amongst the sky, the brightest ones are not the most talented people, or the happiest, or the most perseverant, but the ones who suffer the most that shine brighter than those before and after them. When you read this collection you will see, feel, and know what it
takes to be the brightest star in these
dark skies, for they endure life for endurance, not just for it to pass.

EXPERIMENTAL POEMS

EXCITEMENT

Excitement is a lovely place to be.
The world in that of itself elated.
It's when we live at our highest degree.

That's when we all run wild ourselves to see
us believe that despite being hated.
This place is for you and me that we live.

Jumping for joy from the top of a tree
Shows that my excitement's sure inflated.
Where the body blossoms, the soul is free.

The win races too, I'm amped up, ya see?
Call me naïve or plain antiquated,
This will soon benefit everybody.

Whether or not you're glad or unhappy,
jovial, braggadocio, jaded,
but excitement has no authority.

If you happen to live unhappily,
Speak your truth before your speech is faded.
Let your gums flap and body language flee
from disgust so you'll live more merrily.

FREIGHT TRAIN

The freight train speeds with great authority.
Hundreds of miles of rambunctious action,
with bone crunching sounds of velocity.

The conductor's full of insanity,
as the passengers met with distraction,
Scared to death, yell out loud profanities.

While the endless roaring atrocity
heads towards the barricade, my faction
of friends suffer from its intensity.

For which I pray for inner harmony,
I think that we'll die by many fractions.
Hanging onto the hand strap intensely.

Made me puke! My stomach hurt painfully
while the train began to lose its traction.
We crashed through the barricade, harmfully.

Into the air for the whole world to see.
Recorded on my phone with bad intentions.
Ten cars take a nose dive into sea.
While we've failed to survive...means we're still free.

HEAVY METAL

Heavy metal is great to listen to.
Loud and strong tunes filled with such heart and soul.
Listening to it will help you get through.

the difficulties that make you feel blue.
bigger than a supersized popcorn bowl,
Listen to some Pantera with your crew.

Iron Maiden, Slayer, Lamb of God too.
Throw some Gojira to fill you up whole.
Crank it to the max while clean in your room.

How many more albums can you accrue
before your bank account takes its worst toll?
With stacks of CDs crammed in your bedroom.

Heavy guitars, rattling drums, fun for you.
Remembering those songs, you're on a roll.
Fuck your homework, this is better to do.

Practice your shredding and the basics, too.
One day you might play at the Super Bowl.
Rockin' 'round the world in a year or two
can make you a star right out of the blue.

SUNSET ON THE BEACH

A sunset gives the sky an orange glow,
in the late afternoon, where seagulls squeak.
Chirping away, they all fly in a row.

Beach goers pack up and get set to go.
As this beautiful day has passed its peak,
they gather their belongings far too slow.

Logging from R and R from head to toe
to head to the beach house as their bones creek
for some more rest while watching TV shows.

Children run while the lifeguard's whistle blows
for all to get outta dodge. We all seek
for this salvation with each day we grow.

Only as we grasp for this, we all know
that banality awaits, so very bleak
where one day, we'll be back, but we must go.

Back to the world that makes us hurl and groan.
Those who can't afford this, must feel so weak,
as they want this life, but this is no show.
It ain't no beach, rich or poor, friend or foe.

EMBEDDED SPIRITS

Merging spirits come together as one
to share how they feel in the name of love.
Intertwining the fluids just for fun.

Doesn't make them stronger by the ton.
Instead, flying together, dove to dove,
gives them the care that their congregation

witness Bonnie and Clyde on the run.
They both become one when push comes to shove.
Those who face them will taste lead from their guns.

As a couple faces the world like none
other ever will, look from up above
because as they fly under the hot sun.

They absorb the warmth comforted as one,
transformed to firehawks out from a stove.
To defy the predators 'till they're done.

Eying their surroundings while on the hunt,
in order to see the life in face of
harm where its heavenly features up front
are designed to trick them with guile and brunt.

OBLIVIOUS WORLD

Sad times usually come when we least
expect them to. Sometimes they're just watching
us. Even when we're having a big feast.

The saddest times more fearsome than a beast
are when you can't understand those talking
to you. Communication seems to cease,

even when our conversations increase.
Over the phone, face to face, or speaking
in tongues by text even, wavelengths decrease.

When social cues arise, my soul deceased
as I don't understand hucksters hustling
me. My mind is twisted at ninety degrees.

Not knowing what's true or false, west or east,
north or south, up and down, I am seeing
the concrete melt beneath me like a priest

as if I'm falling in hell where at least
I can confront my worst nightmares, flaming
hot as talking to others...it's a beast.
This is my great obstacle at the least.

HARDCORE

I carry a garbage can of a heart
in my rib cage, which makes me walk so slow,
walking as if I've been falling apart.

Wondering when the first piece will soon part,
my body is strong enough, ready to go.
Into the king-sized cage, when's this match start?

I've waited all day to display my art,
as the clock ticks away for the big show.
In his own locker with a shopping cart,

a baseball bat, thumb tacks, all from Wal-Mart
sits a crazy man, with some steam to blow,
creepy thoughts and an arch rival to thwart.

I'm bringing my casket before we start.
This is your funeral, not some side show.
Bring all your weapons, most of all your heart.

The Garden faithful, in his great landmark,
await this match, between us deranged foes,
looking forward for this swingout to start,
as we set the stage for our heart-to-heart.

ON THE BRINK OF DISASTER

Wired with no limit to stay awake,
my mind is more alive than your soul's dead.
Spinning in my head are dreams of the fake.

Sunny weather with a house by the lake,
along with the bigwigs I come to dread
in order to maintain this life I take

for granted, I groan with a thud and break
into tears, crying that lake of words said
to shaking my guts like a bad earthquake.

Wolves in sheep skin keep me up for Christ's sake.
With their phone calls where others would drop dead.
Listening to the complaints that they make.

I debate whether or not I should flake
or I should feed into the shit I'm fed
that screwing your clients where I just ache.

I've considered all the abuse I take,
I can afford to buy a gun instead,
so I blow my brain fragments in the lake,
as I've had enough of this life to take.

SPENT

Durable through dog days and pitch-black nights,
lives a man whose insomnia awaits him,
while he endures brute pain in these long fights.

He rolls like a pig in mud, to new heights.
He can't sleep, that's one thing…he's so damn grim.
He doesn't care which way is left and right.

The heights reach high orbit as he takes flight,
flying each hour during all these dim
times, where it's when his mind ignites the fright

that takes over his night. The tension's tight
where he storms downstairs as his tensed-up limbs
make for loud footsteps and so erudite

in his awareness, he rambles on right
as he calls the Warmline, eating Slim Jim,
complaining about his problem, his bright

disposition an adrenalin light
up the living room while fatigue calms him
down. He finally falls asleep…good night.
His day ends with, but not without a fight.

INSOMNIA

Alone in my bed with nothing to do,
but turn around all over my mattress,
with sheets slipping off and the sky dark blue.

It's a matter of when I make up to
a day filled with grogginess, nothing less,
but hoping for a fast day to get through.

With heavy eyes and weakened limbs to boot,
I roll up to sit, and I must confess,
I might just call out. With a report due

and a promotion at stake, between you
and me, this may sure deter my success.
As each second ticks away, fortitude

is what I must depend on because soon,
my timeout in this building, with this stress
as well as this world, portraying a zoo,

will dwindle as I dwell on what to do.
Another sleepless night makes me regress,
as insomnia reigns — it's nuthin' new,
as I remain awake without a clue.

ANOTHER OVERNIGHT SHIFT AT CVS

In the overnight, where the skells come out,
the stacks of totes that I set to the side
of the aisles tower, I'm drenched with deep doubt.

Wondering how I'm gonna do without
my night crew members as I'm forced to ride
solo, I shudder inside with a bout

of anxiety. As I feat big crowds
up with butterflies, I just want to hide.
As the customers, coming in and out

of the store start a commotion, right out
of nowhere, I breathe rapidly. Aside
from the truck delivery and totes, South

from the pharmacy, a hooker comes about.
Wearing a peacoat, but nothing to hide
but her backside. She goes lookin' for trout

in the frozen food freezer when a shout
up front alarms me further. I go fly
to the register as a SEAL knocks out
a thug. With blood on the rug, I walk out.

GOOD VS. EVIL

Underground resides a figure of doom.
A dark angel known to all as a demon,
could make all comers cringe in any room.

Features of brute strength that makes a loud boom,
plotting domination for each season,
Could make all comers cringe in any room.

When Jesus rose from the dead from his tomb,
this warlord of evil wasn't leavin',
as his mystique lives for more than a few.

To turn us mere Earthlings into his goons
and burn this planet that leaves you screamin',
with boiling lava that would melt the moon.

There are people who will find out real soon
that with God's deep love, hell will be freezin'
with a chill so cold we'll witness iced gloom.

This spiritual fight comes with a boom.
The two lords come to fight, Earth is beamin'
with authority, as we try to broom
away darkness, picking sides also looms.

THE NEW BREED

You can map out all the plans that you want,
but that doesn't mean you'll get anywhere.
As brave as you may be, scarcity haunts

just about anyone. The many taunt
the people who dream big and never care
how that affects others. They come and flaunt

their jocularity to break their staunch
character. These are foes who don't play fare,
undercutting their prey until they're gaunt

in morale. Their conduct includes clear raunch.
With cheap smuttiness, their style is so rare
that they ruggedly stifle, rudely haunt.

To scare those who stand against them. They want
nothing, but to win, but their rivals stare
at them, they're wondering about a rant.

With a filthy approach, they live to haunt
the establishment as they come to dare,
defy the world with such shock and great daunt.
Playing to win is merely just to want.

UNDERGROUND SHOCK ROCKER

Buried in blood with rugged debonair,
rolling in feces and possibly mud.
Abused and maligned with a pain so rare.

From a lifetime of writhing stings, beware!
Shock rock so tame in a world of such crud,
he'll shit on your head with one grimy stare.

Beating himself up right into despair.
Right through the stage, he's no pop star or stud.
Each night in other towns, he loved to wear

bodily fluids with reason and care.
Because he worked so hard, he was no dud.
He was like a dirty bathroom, with flair.

He was bolder than most rock stars, no fair
that he didn't become bigger, he would
wreck himself so bad, you better be scared.

From digging graves for his parents, how rare
to robbing houses like an outlaw should.
Look out! Dead for decades, it's only fair
to say...GG Allin had lots to share.

A POEM ABOUT WORKLIKE BULLSHIT

In a place where speaking makes one man think,
whose actions speak for him, "Where is my place
in this loud land?", where they can only blink

my eyes once just to see the others sink
their teeth in conversation. Their own space
disappears crowded by talking heads. Stink

fests predicated by bad breath can shrink
anyone's energy. In the rat race
where communication makes others drink.

Give 'em a shot of vodka. On the brink
of a meltdown, a Sinebrychoff. In face
of a crisis, some IPA. They wink

in the mirror, in public, they all sink.
When it's their turn to talk. They state their case,
nursing a hole in their stomach. The dink

who writes their check should see how they must think
when they see a swarm of fast talkers waste
the day talking about the game. The kinks
in their social being leaves them extinct.

TO LIVE

Youth is a lovely phase that we all strive
with a look around their environment
that forces us to grow where all we give

is our being, free will, and a drive
where when we run into trouble, we vent
to show ourselves and others we're alive.

Most people have been steely-eyed since five
while others had vigor that came and went.
Unless you've been livin' in a bee hive,

You would know that youth and vigor derive
from what you love. Young or old, the love sent
to you from the inner spirits that live

more than we do sometimes. People can jive
and rationale about all the time lent
to them that they wasted saying that "I've

got no time for this or that." Those are knives
in the soul...unless we're able to rent
extra time to do more...we'll have arrived,
when we look back to say "We all survived!"

FAWNED BY A CRUSH

When you like someone, your heart should explode.
It should burst out blood leaving you to hack,
Wheeze and throw up just like shooting a load.

out your mouth. When you're in a fearful mode,
and your crush is in the room, and your lack
of consciousness traps you, you're on a road

of turbulence where your yap's shut and sewed
up that come spikes in your gut through your back.
Living with that lump inside of your throat

And your nerves jumpin', everything has slowed
down. Basic life is where to go. Off track
and no place to go, your world wants to goad.

you into this fear you live in. The ode
inside of you that's locked up with no crack
to escape through will stay there with no road

to the outside. Unless you can break the code
that will award you the honor that goads
our world to face times like this will have showed
our lesser selves that we must not erode.

VILLANELLE POEMS

I CAN'T SAY "NO".

I just discovered that I can't say "no".
There's all these things that I don't want to do.
They take my life away so I can't go.

The decisions I make won't let me grow,
As I pick different things I can't do.
I just discovered that I can't say "no".

I should do something that makes my heart glow.
Instead I do demeaning things for you.
They take my life away so I can't go.

Doing things for others don't always show
they'll do it for you. That's how you get screwed.
I just discovered that I can't say "no"

Tough decisions can be your friend or foe.
Surprising you at their worst out of the blue.
They take my life away so I can't go.

Being bound by the universe hurts so
much that there's nothing else that you can choose
I just discovered that I can't say "no".
They take my life away so I can't go.

ROCKIN' THE LEATHER

Rockin' the leather en route to Starland.
There's a metal show out in Sayreville.
The Jersey crowd united, hand in hand.

Bangin' your head to your favorite band,
as they perform on stage with seething will.
Rockin' the leather en route to Starland.

Bring your passion in the pit, don't just stand.
At intermission, grab a brew and chill.
The Jersey crowd united, hand in hand.

When crappy music is played, take a stand.
Don't listen to that station! You get killed!
Rockin' the leather en route to Starland!

Metal, rock and emo are in demand.
Four hours of loud music, what a thrill!
The Jersey crowd united, hand in hand.

Heavy guitars and drums are what the fans
want. All that and a great voice take high skill.
Rockin' the leather en route to Starland.
The Jersey crowd united, hand in hand.

DARK CLOUDS, HEAVY WINDS, AND TEARS OF SORROW

Dark clouds, heavy winds and tears of sorrow.
They represent the future of the rich.
We don't need you pigs to build tomorrow.

Do you have spare cash for us to borrow?
As hard as we work, our life's still a bitch.
Dark clouds, heavy winds and tears of sorrow.

Paid too little with our pride to swallow
leaves our hearts and souls in one, giant stitch.
We don't need you pigs to build tomorrow.

People of power are far too shallow
Homeless people need your help...flip the switch.
Dark clouds, heavy winds, and tears of sorrow.

Elites put on a fake act...so hollow.
They make far too much on some lame ad pitch.
We don't need you pigs to build tomorrow.

What leaders' model can we all follow?
There are so many to choose from...but which?
Dark clouds, heavy winds and tears of sorrow.
We don't need you pigs to build tomorrow.

THE PEACEMAKER

It's a gun. She calls it "The Peacemaker".
When she pulls the gun out, your mouth is shut.
With this gun in hand, nothing can shake her.

Even when gossip gets her in a rut,
a crack shot with this gun, don't mistake her.
It's a gun. She calls it "The Peacemaker".

She knows exactly what she must fight for.
To use this in public, she's half a nut.
With this gun in hand, nothing can shake her.

She knows what "the shit" means, she's been to war.
Without this, she still gun fights with more guts.
It's a gun. I call it "The Peacemaker."

If you fuck around, you'll meet your maker.
She'll shove the Peacemaker right up your butt.
With this gun in hand, nothing can shake her.

She's brutally honest. She's no faker.
In a fight, she'll shut you down like a duck.
It's a gun. It's called "The Peacemaker".
With this gun in hand, nothing can shake her.

SANITY IS BAD FOR THE SPIRIT

Sanity means that you're a bland fuck.
Carving a gimmick to block the carnage.
Immerse yourself in chaos. It saves you.

To be insane means you don't give a fuck,
to practice ruthlessness, to cause damage.
Sanity means that you're just a bland fuck.

To live harmoniously can plain suck!
Live depression living in Anchorage.
Immerse yourself in chaos. It saves you.

Without heart of passion, life runs amok
On those with no culture who are famished
Sanity means that you're just a blank fuck.

Starving for vigor without any luck,
the only way for some is a rampage.
Immerse yourself in chaos. It saves you.

Like getting hit in the face with a puck.
Beats living in vain with a "nice" image.
Sanity means that you're just a bland fuck.
Immerse yourself in chaos. It saves you.

TO KISS OR KILL

Sometimes, it's hard to make a decision,
whether to get a job or create one.
We become what we choose, to kiss or kill.

Everyone of us has a clear vision.
It's better than world leaders who have none.
Sometimes it's hard to make a decision.

To act on this takes a great precision.
To think on your own is better than fun.
We become what we choose, or kiss or tell.

To instill your ideas take friction.
Fight hard for your own destiny, don't run!
Sometimes, it's hard to make a decision.

Whether you're alone or form a legion,
to carry out your greater good as one.
We become what we choose, to kiss or kill.

Spread the great word in every region.
Only together, we can get it done.
Sometimes it's hard to make a decision.
We become what we choose, to kiss or kill.

THE REAL DEVIL

Who exactly is the real devil here?
Regardless of if it's God or Satan,
he comes and stays with us in many forms.

Which direction is it that we'll all steer
to which we'll all seal our brutal fate in?
Who exactly is the real deal here?

Which one's message of the two's crystal clear,
where we decide whose world we can stay in?
He comes and stays with us in many forms.

Which spirit is watching us from the rear,
where what we do is the bed we lay in?
Who exactly is the real devil here?

Who should we choose to worship you without fear?
Who should we all choose without delaying?
He comes and stays with us in many forms.

Will anyone with a wholesome veneer
ever let us know who they're portraying?
Who exactly is the real devil here?
He comes and stays with us in many forms.

THE SHOCK

I love her so much, it hurts to tell her.
Waiting for me to deliver the news.
She looks up at me where she sees "the shock".

The feelings are the worst that have occurred.
Since I last felt this way and it's no cruise.
I love her so much, it hurts to tell her.

My midsection hurts worse than if I were
punched in the stomach shaking in my shoes.
She looks up at me where she sees "the shock".

I left her hanging as I wasn't sure
what to say, even with nothing to lose.
I love her so much, it hurts to tell her.

While looking in her eyes, she was a blur.
Growing impatient, she sees it all through.
She looks up at me where she sees "the shock".

She finally walks, leaving my obscure
blankness to contemplate what else to do.
I love her so much, it hurts to tell her.
She looks up at me when she sees "the shock".

LOVE IS A MENTAL HEALTH ISSUE FOR ALL

Love is a mental health issue for all.
It clouds our judgment as we don't think straight.
Love begins with a fear we all withhold.

Your attention span makes you hit a wall,
it leaves you in a meditative state.
Love is a mental health issue for all.

You grow spikes in your heart, where as you fall,
for someone special, your spirit's irate
Love begins with a fear we all withhold.

As soon as you feel your heart pound, don't stall.
Address these emotions to seal your fate.
Love is a mental health issue for all.

Your psyche runs as fast as it can crawl
in circles. Your call for deep help can't wait.
Love begins with a fear we all withhold.

Overthinking will hurt in the long haul,
where you must emote to open that gate.
Love is a mental health issue for all.
Love begins with a fear we all withhold.

IT'S NEVER "I", IT'S ALWAYS "WE"

A team never says "I": it's always "we".
We always stick together, no matter what.
It's always teamwork that makes the dream work!

As one, we will do things others won't see.
We may not always claim victory but...
A team never says "I". It's always "we".

To win at all cost, it's never for free.
We huddle for strategy and input.
It's always teamwork that makes the dream work!

To be the best yet comes with a steep fee.
For elite status, we run the gauntlet.
A team never says "I". It's always "we".

Playing as a whole unit to a tea.
Our mission's to win and to undercut.
It's always teamwork that makes the dream work!

I will fight for you if you fight for me.
With that said, no doubt we'll reach the summit!
A team never says "I". It's always "we".
It's always teamwork that makes the dream work!

THE FROZEN POND

The frozen pond is where it all begins.
In this tundra, there's no sponsors, no crowd.
Just you and your friends in the bitter cold.

Much to the new neighborhood kid's chagrin,
check him out of his skates out there real loud!
The frozen pond is where it all begins.

If you can hang with them, you're in like Flynn.
Make sure the ice doesn't melt or you'll drown.
Just you and your friends in the bitter cold.

It's where you develop the will to win,
to stare down challenges that make you proud.
The frozen pond is where it all begins.

Live out your fantasy, but play to win,
as this great game has been made to astound,
Just you and your friends in the bitter cold.

To give less than your best is a great sin
because over your head will like dark clouds.
The frozen pond is where it all begins.
Just you and your friends in the bitter cold.

THE MOUNTAINS

Looking up at the mountains, what a treat!
Face to face, I boldly climb with purpose.
To reach the top is to defy yourself.

Not everyone can pursue this great feat.
It's a tough road, don't forget your compass.
Looking up at the mountains, what a treat!

When you reach the top is when you can eat.
Right now, it's time to sweat for your solace.
To reach the top is to defy yourself.

If you're not up to the task, take a seat.
Guaranteed you might land on your carcass!
Looking up at the mountains, what a treat!

When crisis comes, don't give in to defeat.
Doing this don't even scratch the surface.
To reach the top is to defy yourself.

If you fall off, make sure it's on your feet.
Young or old, no matter what day it is!
Looking up at the mountains, what a treat!
To reach the top is to defy yourself.

NO SECURITY IN THE WORLD

There's no security in my own world.
Where I'm going to end up is scary.
Everything is so unpredictable.

With all the intensity that I've hurled,
I live a life that can be so weary.
There's no security in my world.

This live we live is one giant pearl,
gleaming with beauty while weak and dreamy.
Everything is so unpredictable.

Feeling like doing endless bicep curls,
with no end in sight, the muscles burn me.
There's no security in my own world.

My mind's in shambles wired and twirled,
where deep inside there's greatness within me.
Everything is so unpredictable.

There's so much we endure in our own world.
When we come to play, we hide under trees.
There's no security in our own world.
Everything is so unpredictable.

CRYING IS A ROOM OF PIERCING EYEBALLS

Crying is a room of piercing eyeballs,
where you feel watched while trying to stay strong.
Feelings attack us where we can't see them.

Sometimes, my emotions hide behind walls.
Where somewhere down the road, they won't for long.
Crying is a room of piercing eyeballs.

Soon enough, those tears drop like waterfalls,
from the journey traveled with sharp end prongs.
Feelings attack us where we can't see them.

There are many people who hide and crawl,
withholding how they feel for far too long.
Crying is a room of piercing eyeballs.

Your soul endures deep, personal brawls,
to settle past discretions, faults, and wrongs.
Feelings attack us where we can't see them.

Through the unearthed bravery of it all,
they share with a safer crowd their sad song.
Crying is a room of piercing eyeballs.
Feelings attack us where we can't see them.

HEAVY HEARTS

Heavy hearts have more baggage than you think.
Carrying weight so big that they can't walk.
The weight of the world is in all our hearts.

There are days where it's even hard to blink
and my jaw's so still, I can't even talk.
Heavy hearts have more baggage than you think.

On some dark nights, I write without much ink,
where I put out my soul, I can't even talk.
The weight of the world is in all our hearts.

There are days where it's even hard to blink,
and my jaw's so still, I can't even talk.
Heavy hearts have more baggage than you think.

I carry my scars while I'm on the brink,
as our world carries the rest of the bulk.
The weight of the world is in all our hearts.

I hang my big head right over the sink
after work pretending to be the Hulk.
Heavy hearts have more baggage than you think.
The weight of the world is in all our hearts.

MY FEAR FOLLOWS ME

Wherever I go, my fear follows me.
Just when I think it's safe, I end up scared.
The only way out of this pain is through.

This honor is far as the eye could see.
Worried about the worst, always beware.
Wherever I go, my fear follows me.

There are days that I'm brave, some that I flee.
I always need help, and no one is there.
The only way out of this pain is through.

I wish the Boogeyman would leave me be,
but his killer instinct comes without fear.
Whenever I go, my fear follows me.

I kneel on barbed wire for all to see.
To demonstrate my threshold everywhere.
The only way of this pain is through.

I see his shadow hiding from the tree.
He finds me hiding with a chilling stare.
Wherever I go, my fear follows me.
The only way out of this pain is through.

THAT THUNDERING FEELING

Love's a thundering feeling to hold dear.
It takes over your mind, body and soul.
It feels so hard that its pain turns me deaf.

A bongo beating heart is always near.
It pounds my chest looking to form a hole.
Love's a thundering feeling to hold dear.

The world knows that I love you loud and clear
Because the world hears it beat as a whole.
It feels so hard that its pain turns you deaf.

Love occupies me so that I can't hear.
While talking to you, using rigmarole.
Love is a thundering feeling to hold dear.

It even affects the way that I steer
the wheel o' my car heading for a stroll.
It feels so hard that its pain turns you deaf.

It becomes a kryptonite as the sheer
friction of these feelings are hot as coal.
Love's a thundering feeling to hold dear.
It feels so hard that its pain turns you deaf.

A DRAG TO SMILE

Sometimes it's a drag to smile when you can't.
To put on a façade when hardest hit.
To die with a grin is an anathema.

Listening to people schmooze, charm, and rant,
while you nod and chuckle at their bullshit.
Sometimes it's a drug to smile when you can't.

When you lie to yourself, it makes you pant
until you snap and scream out loud, "THAT'S IT!!"
To die with a grin is anathema.

You get so upset that you want to plant
them in the face until their face is split.
Sometimes it's a drag to smile when you can't.

Staying calm with a thick skin doesn't grant
you serenity whenever seen fit.
To die with a grin is anathema.

Being too meek squashes you like an ant.
Stand up and fight back when you want to sit.
Sometimes it's a drag to smile when you can't.
To die without a grin is anathema.

WANNA LOSE MY MIND

There are days where I want to lose my mind.
To scoff at the norm to live in the now.
Reckless living reveals our painful truths.

Sometimes in a world that's so rarely kind,
it's better to cut loose instead of bow.
There are days where I want to lose my mind.

Without a strong moxie, you'll fall behind
on a grand stage where no one will kowtow.
Reckless living reveals our painful truths.

To live authentically means we must grind
while clashing with life with a thud and pow.
There are days where I want to lose my mind.

Sometimes, though, brash or graceful, you'll all find
that any big move is risky somehow.
Reckless living reveals our painful truths.

Even with both eyes open, we're all blind
that the world can shovel us with one plow.
There are days where I want to lose my mind.
Reckless living reveals our painful truths.

SOMETIMES THE WORLD'S NOT READY FOR YOU

Sometimes the world's just not ready for you.
Whether you're ahead or behind its time.
The world wants nothing to do with you.

There's days where people want nothing to do
with you or space which you want to chime.
Sometimes the world's just not ready for you.

There issues make many people feel blue,
when on the ladder in which we all climb.
The world wants not a thing to do with you.

No matter what talents that you accrue,
most prefer some yuppie shit piece of slime.
Sometimes the world's just not ready for you.

I work hard and have skill, but have no clue
why I can't make real cash much less a dime.
This world wants not a thing to do with you.

No matter how much I'm out there, they shoo
me a way as if they don't have much time.
Sometimes the world's just not ready for you.
This world wants to a thing to do with you.

EXHAUSTED ALONE

Exhausted alone with a lively mind.
My mind is alive with each racing thought.
Everything I go through is in my head.

Each day is an adventure that's not kind
where my brain burns with thoughts that make me rot.
Exhausted alone with a lovely mind.

It's every day in my active mind
where I meet my critic, like it or not.
Exhausted alone with a lively mind.

In all of my cells, I will always find
something wrong with me that gets me so hot.
Exhausted alone with a lively mind.

"You can't do it!" and "You must!" intertwine
while I dream of victory quite a lot.
Everything I got through is in my head.

Daydreaming, though, always leaves me behind,
where I forget about things I forgot.
Exhausted alone with a lively mind.
Everything I go through is in my head.

THERE ARE DAY WHERE I FEEL LIKE KILLING YOU

There are days where I feel like killing you.
You've fucked around with me for way too long.
To fuck with me means to be just like me.

The pressure I face that you have no clue
about will empower me to prove you wrong.
There are days where I feel like killing you.

My resolve is fresh, but I still get blue
over the bad things you said all along.
There are days where I feel like killing you.

For every scar on my back and shoe
in my gut. To say that I'm done is wrong.
There are days where I feel like killing you.

The world don't know shit about what to do.
Fight back while being beaten down by King Kong.
To fuck with me means to be just like me.

Been bulletproof for each word that's gone through
my stomach like enduring a bad pop song.
There are days where I feel like killing you.
To fuck with me means to be just like me.

STRONG WHILE WEAK

It's human to think you're strong when you're weak.
You beat your chest when you want to die.
Strong and weak intertwine where you lose track.

Like when a cancer patient feels so meek.
and their steadfast demeanor is alive.
It's human to think you're strong when you're weak.

Your back's to the wall and you're up shit's creek.
But you wink at Satan when you should cry.
Strong and weak intertwine when you lose track.

Waking up gaunt and pale, your life's lookin' bleak,
Yet your facade is one that no one will deny.
It's human to think you're strong when you're weak.

There are sad times when you're lost and you seek
the joy while hurting as the time ticks by.
Strong and weak intertwine when you lose track.

Where life's obstacles baffles the most sleek
where life in itself makes you wonder why.
It's human to think you're strong when you're weak.
Strong and weak intertwine when you lose track.

THAT SHIT HURT

I'm glad it's over, 'cuz boy, that shit hurt!
Patiently fighting while utterly sore.
Living through discomfort kills you slowly.

Walking in the park while writhing in dirt.
As I cling to life battling to the core.
I'm glad it's over, 'cuz boy, that shit hurt!

With every limb in pain, I get curt
with the notion of what I'm living for.
Living through discomfort kills you slowly.

This struggle strips me of all but the shirt
on my back as the pain turns into gore.
I'm glad it's over, 'cuz boy, that shit hurt!

With atrophied vigor, I'm more alert
that the end is near and death is in store.
Living through discomfort kills you slowly.

The less I care about my health, I'll flirt
with a delayed death that I've prepared for.
I'm glad it's over, 'cuz boy, that shit hurt!
Living through discomfort kills you slowly.

OWEN 3:16 SAYS "I JUST BROKE YOUR NECK."

Owen 3:16: I just broke your neck.
You mess with me, I'll drop you on the mat.
Watch out for your head. I'm gonna spike it.

From Calgary all the way to Quebec,
from the Maritimes to Medicine Hat.
Owen 3:16: I just broke your neck.

When I climb into the ring, hit the deck.
I'll bring you down in just two seconds flat.
Watch out for your head. I'm gonna spike it.

If you shoot with me, I'll leave you a wreck,
as I'll impose my will right off the bat.
Owen 3:16: I just broke your neck.

I'll beat yer ass with a napkin, a deck
of playing cards, or chair on which you sat.
Watch out for your head, I'm gonna spike it.

When I drop your head straight down, not one speck
of you will move, whether skinny or fat.
Owen 3:16: I just broke your neck.
Watch out for your head. I'm gonna spike it.

LOVE AND LUST INTERTWINE

Sometimes love and lust can go together.
Your heart reaches for her with its loud beats.
You're touched by beauty, but long for that thrill.

You want this moment, but then another,
which won't settle, you scream for more feats.
Sometimes love and lust can go together.

A kiss can lead to deep passions farther
than expected as your tension depletes.
You're touched by beauty, but long for that thrill.

The excitement they have lets them rather
ravage each other in a room of heat.
Sometimes love and lust can go together.

There's a small spritz of love with a harder
desire that sweep them right off their feet.
Your touched by beauty, but long for that thrill.

Home from a hard work day, hot and bothered,
needing to express what you can't delete.
Sometimes love and lust can go together.
You're touched by beauty, but long for that thrill.

JUST ONE CHANCE AT LOVE

Give me a chance to love you sincerely.
I'll showcase my grace alongside great flair.
Let me show you the right way one should love.

Do I think that you're hot? Definitely!
But I'll demonstrate how I deeply care.
Give me a chance to love you sincerely.

Most men want you, but they don't remotely
think about feelings or care to be aware.
Let me show you the right way one should love.

Most men want you but they don't remotely
think about feeling or care to be aware.
Give me a chance to love you sincerely.

Living single is tranquil as can be,
but high rent with love have lots more to share.
Let me show you the right way one should love.

These feelings are so strong that I can't flee,
sharing our deep fears requires a pair.
Give me a chance to love you sincerely.
Let me show you the right way one should love.

HEAVY EYES

Drowsiness is a spell that wastes my time.
I feel like sleeping when I just wanna write.
I just wonder if I'll die in my sleep.

On days where I'm out, things drop on a dime
and I get so sleepy, I lose my might.
Drowsiness is a spell that wastes my time.

On days where I have errands, it's a crime
to be tired to stay awake. I must fight.
I just wonder if I'll die in my sleep.

My body wears down as it feels like slime.
Time to fall asleep, the time's about right.
Drowsiness is a spell that wastes my time.

To be tuckered out all day leaves behind
a life worth living as day turns to night.
I just wonder if I'll die in my sleep.

If I can muster the time to align
my Circadian rhythm, I'll take flight.
Drowsiness is a spell that wastes my time.
I just wonder if I'll die in my sleep.

EVERYTHING IS FAKE

Everything is fake. The world is fiction.
Everything we have is an illusion.
Even if it's real, life's a king-sized dream.

When I deal with people, there's some friction.
The only real things are its contusions.
Everything is fake. The world is fiction.

Our soul's became inner apparitions,
where the most real spirits cause confusion.
Even if it's real, life's a king-sized dream.

The voices in my head cause affliction
where the thought of "can't" is an illusion.
Everything is fake. The world is fiction.

From money to mailboxes, depictions
like them is the mind's trippiest soothing.
Even if it's real, life's a king-sized dream.

The world lives as so, but takes no action.
in causing a woke "fake world" invasion.
Everything is fake, the world is fiction.
Even if it's real, life's a king-sized dream.

A STILL BEATING HEART

My still heart beats for you when it shouldn't.
You find me to be handsome, but awkward.
I still love you and how you make me feel.

I'd throw myself in hell for you. Couldn't
you at least respect me moving forward?
My heart still beats for you when it shouldn't.

I'd kill myself for you, but I wouldn't
want you to slip on gooey blood, Good Lord!
I still love you and how you make me feel.

I know that you don't love me back. Couldn't
be the women in the past that I've whored?
My heart still beats for you when it shouldn't.

My feelings now hurt, were in the most mint
condition 'til you hurt them where I roared.
I still love you and how you make me feel.

Don't play games with me. I could take a hint.
When you twist your words, I start to get bored.
My heart still beats for you when it shouldn't,
I still love you and how you make me feel.

SUPERMODEL SATAN

The devil looks like a supermodel.
Hotter than hell but burns you at the stake.
Watch out for those babes, even the sizzlers.

I saw one girl that made my heart throttle.
She looked so hot, but her assets were fake.
The devil looks like a supermodel.

When I went to reach for my wine bottle,
the model greeted me with sirloin steak.
Watch out for those babes, even the sizzlers.

Her sincerity and great charm coddled
me with a massage, sex, and then more cake.
The devil looks like a supermodel.

Just as the model went to go fondle
me. I felt a rush of puke from that steak.
Watch out for those babes, even the sizzlers.

My throat and chest are hit by the rattled
Effects of the poison I received. Christ's sakes.
The devil looks like a supermodel.
Watch out for those babes, even the sizzlers.

DANCE OF COMBAT

It's always about the dance...always was.
Driving to the arena, rockin' out.
Make them love ya, make them love hatin' ya!

Get ready to watch some staged combat, cuz
It's gonna be a barnburner, no doubt.
It's always about the dance...always was.

The best thing about the crowd is the buzz
as they're revived up for the upcoming bouts.
Make them love ya, make them love hate hatin' ya!

Gearin' up to fight, so watch out because,
makin' people bleed's what I'm all about.
It's always about the dance...always was.

This is a profession where no one else does
nasty like me so you're in for a rout.
Make them love ya, make them love hatin' ya!

When it comes to rasslin', I'm the best there was.
You mess with me, I'm gonna use my clout!
It's always about the dance...always was.
Make them love you, make them love hatin' ya!

SORE AND TIRED

Pain and drowsiness interfere with life.
We all lust for comfort and needless sleep.
We chose to dive when we should live instead.

We jump to conclusions when the big knife
kills us and our momentum we have dead.
Pain and drowsiness interfere with life.

When you're ready to make that crucial dive,
we turn around and go back to our bed.
We all lust for comfort and needless sleep.

This behavior resembles a low life,
as we have down with that comfort ahead.
Pain and drowsiness interfere with life.

The goddesses of silk become the wife
in this marriage of loafing up ahead.
We all lust for comfort and needless sleep.

Looking to alleviate ourselves from strife,
we cling onto pillows in which we wed.
Pain and drowsiness interfere with life
We all lust for comfort and needless sleep.

COMATOSE BY HYPNOTISM

Comatose by hypnotism, we rot.
We're all fazed by sleep and a needed trans.
We give into the desires of sloth.

It's a heavyweight fight, like it or not.
It brings us down to the seat of our pants.
Comatose by hypnotism, we rot.

It's a draining mess, we endure a lot.
With fatigue at large, our slack will enhance.
We give into the desires of sloth.

The pendulum becomes our guide, if not,
a dictator that halts our hopes by chance.
Comatose by hypnotism, we rot.

No matter how hard and ragefully I fought,
I lost my throne with a valiant stance.
We give into the desires of sloth.

The dream of light has now darkened. It's not
clear for us to see our own dreams advance.
Comatose by hypnotism, we rot.
We give into the desires of sloth.

MY HEART IS A JIGSAW PUZZLE

My heart is a rubbled jigsaw puzzle.
I still dwell on the loves that are have-nots.
With each piece broken, my spirit coughs blood.

I can't talk about this as the muzzle
within me can't explain why my soul rots.
My heart is a rubbled jigsaw puzzle.

In the world of love, we gotta hustle,
to express that hole that lies in our guts.
With each piece broken, my spirit coughs blood.

There's no elixir that you can guzzle,
to heal the wounds that put us all in knots.
My heart is a rubbled jigsaw puzzle.

With the damage done that loves gives us all,
sometimes it's best that we're all after thoughts.
With each piece broken, my spirit coughs blood.

Our hearts are really the strongest muscle.
With heartbreak in tow, we take our beset shots.
My heart is a rubbled jigsaw puzzle
With each piece broken, my spirit coughs blood.

ROAR WITH REASON

Steaming from the past, I roar with reason.
It's time to confront myself, here and now.
It's not how you start, it's how you finish.

For each and every single season.
I live like a sheep dog, but not a cow.
Steaming from the past. I roar with reason.

I've finished a life of people pleasin'.
As I dent the Earth with a BANG and POW!
It's not how you start, it's how you finish.

My new-found courage conquers each region,
with no more shit that I'll ever allow.
Steaming from the past, I roar with reason.

To think I'll bow down, you must be dreamin',
it's time to strike hard and grab the right now.
It's not how you start, it's how you finish.

With a new attitude, life is gleamin'.
Despite hardships, we're a proud land somehow.
Steaming from the past, I roar with reason.
It's not how you start, it's how you finish.

FALL TO RISE

We fall down only to rise up again.
That's the meaning of our own livelihood.
Each day's a gift and a tribulation.

Life can be a fight in the lion's den.
Be armed for battle like anyone should.
We fall down only to rise up again.

We must have enough ink in our pen
to write a proud ending like we all could.
Each day's a gift and a tribulation.

When we suffer greatly, we can't pretend
to wash it all away like others would.
We fall down only to rise up again.

The only people that we can resent
is ourselves for not fighting for all's good.
Each day's a gift and a tribulation.

We must not break down nor should we yield, bend,
or roll over to those of great delude.
We fall down only to rise up again.
Each day is a gift and tribulation.

TO SURF IS TO CLIMB

A big wave to surf is a hill to climb
as we grab our boards to ride that very wave.
To stare down this challenge means we're ready.

For the extreme daredevils, it's your time
to wear that title to show us you're brave.
A big wave to surf is a hill to climb.

The waters are tricky. They'll drop on a dime
as you can fall to your watery grave.
To stare down this challenge means we're ready.

We need all of our own to come and chime
in, to thwart the evil meant to enslave.
A big wave to surf is a hill to climb.

With each day that we face that gives us grime,
we use our power only mortals crave.
To stare down this challenge means we're ready.

We battle this wave who commit the crime
of trying to wipe us off this enclave.
A big wave to surf is a hill to climb.
To stare down this challenge means we're ready.

I WILL FUCK YOU IN THE FACE WITH MY FIST

I will fuck you in the face with my fist.
I will hit you harder than a MAC truck
Your face is an asshole. My fist's a dick!

Better watch your back or you'll make the list.
I'll crack your teeth in, I don't give a fuck.
I will fuck you in the face with my fist.

Goin' toe to toe with me's just a gist
of what darkness is like without no luck.
Your face is an asshole, my fist's a dick!

To goad me, rile me up, or get me pissed
is a corner you're back's against. You're stuck.
I will fuck you in the face with my fist!

I'll accept your offer, if you insist.
Beware my limbs cuz I'll bludgeon you, schmuck.
Your face is an asshole, My fist's a dick!

I'm a headhunter and I never missed.
My skills are so flawless, I'll run amok.
I will fuck you in the face with my fist.
Your face is an asshole, my fist's a dick!

BLOOD OUT OF A ROCK

Punching blood out of a rock's quite a feat!
I can blow up your face with just one punch.
This is the best magic trick of all time.

With hands of stone, I'll be far from defeat.
My power separates me from the bunch.
Punching blood out of a rock's quite a feat!

Don't try to stare me down, dude. Take a seat!
I'll eat you like a shitburger for lunch.
This is the best magic trick of all time.

I can hit so hard, you fly off your feet
and land on your head. Don't call it a hunch!
Punching blood out of a rock's quite a feat!

I'll hit harder that you hit the concrete.
It'll sound like eating a Nestle Crunch.
This is the best magic trick of all time.

Me fightin' you is just another treat.
Your corpse is just food for hoodrats to munch.
Punching blood out of a rock's quite a feat.
This is the best magic trick of all time.

MORE HARM THAN WE NEED

My mind can't stop saying bad things to me.
My feelings are hurting from one dark thought.
We all cause ourselves more harm when we need.

There are days I wanna hide in a tree,
from the brutal battles that I have fought.
My mind can't stop saying bad things to me.

The negative talk I make makes me flee
into pricey therapy that I've bought.
We all cause ourselves more harm than we need.

This nihilistic way of life can be
a terror for all the pain it has brought.
My mind can't stop saying bad things to me.

My whole life as far as the eye can see,
were the best choices that I could have caught.
We all cause ourselves more harm than we need.

Our own meaningless stings like a bee,
for the broken dreams that we all have sought.
My mind can't stop saying bad things to me.
We all cause ourselves more harm than we need.

BLACKLISTED BY A PROSTITUTE

I was blacklisted by a prostitute.
I decided not to have sex somehow.
All 'cuz I didn't want to mate with her.

I should be in a mental institute,
due to the fact that I don't want to plow.
I was blacklisted by a prostitute.

The hooker was middle-aged, not even cute.
She wasn't that pretty, but not a cow.
All 'cuz I didn't want to mate with her.

I had no respect, didn't give a hoot.
I had not regret turnin' down sex somehow.
I was blacklisted by a prostitute.

I had just gotten paid a ton of loot.
I decided not to spend anyhow.
All 'cuz I didn't want to mate with her.

My last-minute choice just gave me the boot.
"You won't fuck here again!", she said aloud.
I was blacklisted by a prostitute.
All 'cuz I didn't want to mate with her.

I FEEL THAT NOBODY LIKES ME

Sometimes I feel that nobody likes me.
On my lonesome where I must stand alone.
Alone in the world with no one around.

I have talent and drive, how could it be
that most people leave me all on my own?
Sometimes I feel that nobody likes me.

There are detractors at a high degree,
where I'm always inside of their red zone.
Alone in the world with no one around.

Everyone around wants to see me flee
to a point where my heart has turned to stone.
Sometimes I feel that nobody likes me.

I always greet people, say niceties,
and smile to hide the scars from which they're sewn.
Alone in the world with no one around.

Bottom line is, no matter who you see,
it's better off sometimes to be alone.
Sometimes I feel that nobody likes me.
Alone in the world with no one around.

THE METAPHYSICS OF BAD LUCK

Bad luck follows me around everywhere.
I try to plan for the good days ahead.
The world of metaphysics deceives me.

There's so much gloom that life will always share,
where for most of us good luck's best of dead.
Bad luck follows me around everywhere.

For people with humility beware,
your fortune's about to go south instead.
The world of metaphysics deceives me.

Valiant efforts vanish in the air,
as it poisons our hopes much worse than lead.
Bad luck follows me around everywhere.

Set a goal or plot a scheme if you dare.
I'll send your greatest dreams to its death bed.
The world of metaphysics deceives me.

Invisible evils are out to declare
war on eudaimonia 'till it's dead.
Bad luck follows me around everywhere.
The world of metaphysics deceives me.

ROAR FOR SERENITY

I need to roar so I can be serene.
I just can't hold it in any longer.
To yell out my discomfort cleans my veins.

My soulful expressions always careen
toward the world to help fend those stronger
I need to roar so I can be serene.

My screams can shatter my own TV screen,
as I fight for peace as a war monger.
To yell out my discomfort cleans my veins.

On the internet or a magazine,
you'll see the carnage of what I stand for.
I need to roar so I can be serene.

Baring my tiger blood like Charlie Sheen,
I growl at injustice with great anger.
To yell out my discomfort cleans my veins.

I release my tension to bust your spleen,
to cleanse my spirit using sheer power.
I need to roar so I can be serene.
To yell out my discomfort cleans my veins.

FRAILTY OF THE HEART

My heart breaks each day just like it's nothin'.
I'm always going through all types of aches.
Some days it breaks in all different spots.

Wake up grabbin' my chest, I'm no bluffin'.
Thought it was a heart attack for Christ's sakes.
My heart breaks each day just like it's nothin'.

This morning, I was huffin' and puffin',
thinkin' I'd die, this was no tummy ache.
Some days it breaks in all different spots.

Maybe this is all from the face stuffin'
I did in my day, pizza, candy, cake...
My heart breaks each day just like it's nothin'.

Maybe it's from the cigarettes I'm puffin'.
Or the loves I ain't had makin' me break.
Some days it breaks in all different spots.

Heartbreak'll turn you into a muffin.
It can numb you to death or make you shake.
My heart breaks each day just like it's it's nothin',
Some days it breaks in all different spots.

FACING LIFE ALONE

Facing life alone is what we all do.
I'm stuck in a world with no assistance.
We all need help, but there's no one around.

Getting kicked in the ass by a big shoe,
doesn't always build your pain resistance.
Facing life alone is what we all do.

This planet has triple teams made for you.
Nobody guards there to keep your distance.
We all need help, but there's no one around.

Brawling in massacres with no street crew,
having no close friends can be a nuisance.
Facing life alone is what we all do.

You're home by yourself fighting with the flu.
Sickness and loneliness have congruence.
We all need help, but there's no one around.

On days where it's everyone versus you,
it's time to carve out your great resilience.
Facing life alone is what we do.
We all need help, but there's no one around.

THE SUN IS WATCHING

The sun always keeps an eye on us all,
as we soak in the rays, we turn to mush.
The summer days keep tabs on all of us.

Making sure the heat doesn't make us fall,
it watches us brace for that epic push.
The sun always has its eye on us all.

It melts our spirit in this outdoor brawl.
The heat it brings doesn't beat around the bush.
The summer days keep tabs on all of us.

This sweltering star backs us to a wall
and takes its time to kill us with no rush.
The sun always has its eye on us all.

As we head to the air-conditioned mall,
we await our death with a serene hush.
The summer days keep tabs on all of us.

As the devil beckons a soulful call,
we answer passed out with a hapless fall.
The sun always has its eye on us all.
The summer days keep tabs on all of us.

SOUL FROM MIND

The soul differentiates from the mind.
I always want, but I need even more.
What the inside burns for, the head forgets.

There are many things that I try to find.
It's the things I need that help make me roar.
The soul differentiates from the mind.

Sometimes our passions can leave us behind.
It's our principles that make us soar.
What the inside burns for, the head forgets.

We give into lust of every kind,
as the needs we have stagnates to bore.
What the inside burns for, the head forgets.

Our mandatory needs are far less kind
than the things we gratify and adore.
What the inside burns for, the head forgets.

Sometimes our needs and wants are intertwined,
as they build us up and strengthen our core.
The soul differentiates from the mind.
What the inside burns for, the head forgets.

A BATTERED SOUL IS A STRONGER MIND

A battered soul is a much stronger mind.
I fight my own evil that pounds my flesh.
This soulful battlefield has made me strong.

This road to power that others can't find
is a foundation for few that stay fresh.
A battered soul is a much stronger mind.

Collectively as one, we all align
to stave off the torture that steals our breath.
This soulful battlefield has made me strong.

To endure the beating is a clean sign
that a broken community can mesh
A battered soul is a much stronger mind.

Together we embrace the deep dark grind
that shows our wounds and wrinkles, nice and fresh.
This soulful battlefield has made me strong.

There's no time for us to rest or unwind.
As war will hit us hard like Eric Esch.
A battered soul is a much stronger mind.
This soulful battlefield has made me strong.

CHAINED TO A BOMB WITH NO SHALLOW END

I'm chained to this bomb, ready to explode.
I want to escape to save my own skin.
There's no shallow end to this massacre.

With death far ahead ready to unload
its wrath. There's a scared little child within.
I'm chained to this bomb, ready to explode.

Looking to save my life on this bleak road,
to blow up in pieces would be a sin.
There's no shallow end to this massacre.

With seconds to go, desperation mode
arrives. My waning moments sink in.
I'm chained to this bomb, ready to explode.

With no intentions to wilt or implode,
I try to cut this steel as time wears thin,
There's no shallow end to this massacre.

This is the end as my life will erode
to blown up organs from the outside in.
I'm chained to this bomb, ready to explode.
There's no shallow end to this massacre.

HAVE MOOD, WILL TRAVEL

My bad mood can travel from place to place.
I'm walking around with this bad feeling.
Don't go near me or you'll also get sick.

In this messiness with the human race,
their lack of empathy gets me reeling.
My bad mood can travel from place to place.

With the anger I showcase on my face,
I share terrible vibes far from healing.
Don't go near me or you'll also get sick.

As people ride me and get on my case,
my skin erodes and endures a peeling.
My bad mood can travel from place to place.

My deep-seated anger is such a waste.
I'll spread it to others and the ceiling.
Don't go near me or you'll also get sick.

As I feel the flames pick up a fast pace,
the fire burns this world without yielding.
My bad mood can travel from place to place.
Don't go near me or you'll also get sick.

THE POTHOLES TO ADVENTURE

Potholes are booby traps to adventure.
Riding place to place for tranquility.
Traveling is a large chore on its own.

Sometimes the travels 'round town are torture.
Its obstacles bring me calamity.
Potholes are booby traps to adventure.

My bumpy road can be a giant lecture,
as my guest on Earth brings nobility.
Traveling is a large chore on its own

Exploring where you live, it's a great venture
to see how to live with monstrosity.
Potholes are booby traps to adventure.

With each image so grateful to capture,
we hardly see life's harshest tyranny.
Traveling is a large chore on its own.

Unlike riding in an elevator,
A read less traveled brings adversity.
Potholes are bobby traps to adventure.
Traveling is a large chore on its own.

THE MELT OF ROMANCE

Romance is so intense, it'll melt you.
When I have feelings, they go far too deep.
I feel so hard for her, it gets scary.

This guest with a partner is something few
people experience, it makes them weep.
Romance is so intense it'll melt you.

It's the one thing in my life that I blew,
as my raw feelings paint me as a creep.
I feel so hard for her, it gets scary.

With each heartbeat, I feel like it just grew
so big and loud enough for me to sleep.
Romance is so intense, it'll melt you.

Hungry eyes and passion are nuthin' new,
while I see my prized piece, I take that leap.
I feel so hard for her, it gets scary.

I'm stuck on you like a big piece of glue,
while you broke my heart in a lifeless heap.
Romance is so intense, it'll melt you.
I feel so hard for her, it gets scary.

THE DREAD OF EXISTENTIAL CHOICE

Doing what we want comes with a grave price.
Sometimes, all we have is to pick and choose.
The decisions we make haunt us surely.

Whether we eat pizza, chicken, or rice,
you are what you eat, want, need...even choose.
Doing what we want comes with a grave price.

Whatever mood we're in, naughty or nice,
can determine destiny, win or lose.
The decisions we make haunt us surely.

Either way, we choose to kill, spear or slice
says a lot, whatever weapon we choose.
Doing what we want comes with a grave price.

Who we all believe in, Satan or Christ,
gives us responsibility to use.
The decisions we use haunt us surely.

No matter how you want to toss the dice,
seven or a snake eyes, you could still lose.
Doing what we want comes with a grave price.
The decisions we use haunt us surely.

STRONG EMOTIONS WEAR YOU OUT

Anger and sadness always wear you out.
These two emotions take such waning tolls.
Negative feelings like these kill people.

They can cause such dread, even when we shout.
They mean the same thing as they break our souls.
Anger and sadness always wear us out.

However, you feel, it makes us all pout,
as they can both play life-altering roles.
Negative feelings like these kill people.

You can cry or growl and lose in a rout,
as these feelings make you walk on hot coals.
Anger and sadness always wear us out.

It can ruin our day or week, no doubt,
when these things are triggered by such assholes.
Negative feelings like these kill people.

They make life a full-blown heavyweight bout,
like running or driving straight into poles.
Anger and sadness always us out.
Negative feelings like these kill people.

THE ONLY WAY OUT: SUICIDE

Sometimes suicide's the only way out.
Living in fear is no way to be free.
Trying to stay alive can still kill you.

These are days I'm unsure what life's about,
what to stand for or even what to be.
Sometimes suicide's the only way out.

Whether or not you have all sorts of clout
or an average schmo that's just like me.
Trying to stay alive can still kill you.

Reach for that gun so I don't see you pout,
as the truth of the bullet sets you free.
Sometimes suicide's the only way out.

Everyone's life can go north or go south,
but when things go bad, you won't want to see.
Trying to stay alive can still kill you.

Staying alive is an option, no doubt,
but your life won't get better, can't ya see?
Sometimes suicide's the only way out,
Trying to stay alive can still kill you.

BIG-TIME BOMB

You turn my heart into a big-time bomb.
Each day that I see you, my heart explodes.
The sweet pain that I feel for you hurts me.

Every time I see you, make no qualms,
that this is a joyride I've never rode.
You turn my heart into a big-time bomb.

I have to breathe too deeply to stay calm
to tell you this feeling I never showed.
This sweet pain that I feel for you hurts me.

Let me hold your hand with my sweaty palm,
as I open my heart to you...behold.
You turn my heart into a big-time bomb.

You make my head spin like a CD-ROM.
I have feelings on my chest to unload.
This sweet pain that I feel for you hurts me.

As I aid my chapped lips with some lip balm,
I get into a brave Prince Charming mode.
You turn my heart into a big-time bomb.
This sweet pain that I feel for you hurts me.

LOOKIN' OUT FOR #1

People care about themselves far too much.
They're always fighting to remain alive.
All they want for themselves is a lot more.

They want more money, prestige, love, and such.
These are the only things, which mortals strive.
People care about themselves far too much.

Selfishness is a societal crutch
that the vibes of purity take a dive.
All they want for themselves is a lot more.

We'll need a lot more than a magic touch,
to give more to this world so we'll survive.
People care about themselves, far too much.

When we need a helping hand in the clutch,
we must all show compassion while we thrive.
All they want for themselves is a lot more.

We don't care about other people much,
but communication keeps us alive.
People care about themselves far too much.
All they want for themselves is a lot more.

LIFE IS A CLUTTER

Life is a clutter when you don't know it.
I don't notice that I can make a mess.
I need to get all my shit together.

Books stacked on the desk with excess bullshit.
I have too much junk here where I need less.
Life is a clutter when you don't know it.

My room's a rollercoaster ride with it
with garbage, dirty clothes, I must confess.
I need to get all my shit together.

When it comes time to clean my room, I sit
and look at how I fix up this duress.
Life is a clutter when you don't know it.

To rearrange my space, which I see fit,
could be the difference to my success.
I need to get all my shit together.

In this place where I sleep, which is a pit,
I will take my time to fight off the stress.
Life is a clutter when you don't know it.
I need to get all my shit together.

MIRACLE OF STRENGTH

My heart is a stronger miracle than you.
With all the hurts I've had, it still beats on.
Resilience shows broken hearts still beat.

The heartbreak and bullshit I go through,
I also adore, but it's far from gone.
My heart is a stronger muscle than you.

Sometimes on strange days, I don't have a clue.
My courage is there and it weighs a ton.
Resilience shows that broken hearts still beat.

We all live in such a dreadful milieu,
that together we share a scarce, deep bond.
My heart is a stronger muscle than you.

Even if you like whatever you do,
shit continues to pile up from here on.
Resilience shows that broken hearts still beat.

We never hide from our true selves or run
our lives of redundancy live on.
My heart is a stronger muscle than you.
Resilience shows that broken hearts still beat.

JOURNEYMAN'S ROAD

A journeyman's road is an odd voyage.
With twists and turns without any road map.
Not every vagabond is homeless.

Wandering around with all this courage,
burnin' fuel to crash for a late night's nap.
A journeyman's road is an odd voyage.

Lookin' for a place to leave your baggage,
but no one wants to put up with your crap.
Not every vagabond is homeless.

Going job to job for minimum wage,
before you're willing to even adapt.
A journeyman's road is an odd voyage.

Eating a price ham and cheese sandwich,
drivin' drunk with a Keystone on my lap.
Not every vagabond is homeless.

Beatin' the streets, roamin' like a savage,
all before lights out to a crisp nightcap.
A journeyman's road is an odd voyage.
Not every vagabond is homeless.

L-O-V-E

Love is just a shitty four-letter word.
It holds weight whether used in love or hate.
People say "I love you" but don't mean it.

The most fucked up thing that I ever heard,
that alone puts too much shit on my plate.
Love is just a shitty four-letter word.

When you try to hang me, I flip the bird
for I have no need to go on a date.
People say "I love you" but don't mean it.

I look out for myself unlike the herd.
I believe in self-care, I'm no cheapskate.
Love is just a shitty four-letter word.

Sometimes "love" just isn't the best choice word.
If you don't show me, it'll be too late.
People say "I love you", but don't mean it.

To prove your love unlike anyone could.
It's a talent that is far from innate.
Love is just a shitty four-letter word.
People say I love you, but don't mean it.

SPLOSH MY BONES

I paid for a splosher to jump my bones.
Once upon a time, seven years ago.
I fell in lust with an ugly beach whale.

It was a ham hock prostitute who was
this one room that I had money to blow.
I paid for a splosher to jump my bones.

She had a beer belly and flabby cones.
I could've said "no", but went with the flow.
I fell in lust with an ugly beach whale.

She sounded clear and decent on the phone,
only to look like a king-sized pillow.
I paid for a splosher to jump my bones.

Instead of paying for my student loans,
I spent my free money on this fat hoe.
I fell in lust with an ugly beach whale.

I shot a smooth one right out of my bones.
It was a quick twenty-two second show.
I paid for a splosher to jump my bones.
I fell in lust with an ugly beach whale.

WANDERIN' 'ROUND THE WORLD

I wander the world, lost for no reason.
There are so many places to explore.
Sometimes we can get lost in our own home.

With all the wandering in each season,
comes nothing, but mass confusion galore.
I wander the world lost for no reason.

Life's no picnic, it's not easy breezin'.
Soul searching is messy with blood and gore.
Sometimes we can get in our own home.

To find your way take your licks and lesions,
but go against the grain at its deep core.
I wander the world lost for no reason.

Life is a king-sized maze for a reason.
To search for meaning and what you stand for.
Sometimes we can get lost in our own home.

Whether you're Joe Schmo or Brendan Gleeson,
search for truth in your life and make it more.
I wander the world lost for no reason.
Sometimes we can get lost in our own home.

CLUELESS

Clueless is an existential being.
My actions get me in so much trouble.
My impulses are ways of true living.

There are times I don't see what I'm doing.
As my mistakes pile up on the double.
Clueless is an existential being.

Always acting, but I'm never seeing
myself as I could fall into rubble.
My impulses are ways of true living.

My unplanned clumsiness is a being
of what we all are out of our bubble.
Clueless in an existential being.

Lack of self-awareness has me seething,
where just one false move will get me pummeled.
My impulses are ways of true living.

Living is an abstract world where being
yourself is a quantum leap or stumble.
Clueless is an existential being.
My impulses are ways of true living.

INVISIBLE FORCES

Invisible forces decide our fate.
We're the ones who act on mind and spirit.
Free will is the strongest power there is.

Environment and action are those that slate,
whether we get smashed or are a smash hit.
Invisible forces decide our fate.

We can take action or be still and wait.
Our destiny's not based on sacred writs.
Free will is the strongest power there is.

Through skill, grit or willpower that's innate,
we all fight predetermined lives that's shit.
Invisible forces decide our fate.

It's love we need before it's all too late,
as we search for our way in life's toolkit.
Free will is the strongest power there is.

We all have one life to live, love and hate.
We must keep our values close by, close knit.
Invisible forces decide our fate.
Free will is the strongest power that is.

A HEART OF GOLD IS A SPIRIT OF PAIN

A heart of gold is a spirit of pain.
As I've been there, done that, as will you.
My iron fist will show you that I care.

It beats louder than life despite its stains.
While down and out, dying, watch what I do.
A heart of gold is a spirit of pain.

Without the pain I give, you'll have no gain.
You'll never experience something new.
My iron fist will show you that I care.

A constant coddling will leave you in chains
when strong direction will give you a clue.
A heart of gold is a spirit of pain.

Open your soul and let me fill your brain
with wisdom and might you'll need to stay true.
My iron fist will show you that I care.

As the world beat us with fiery reign,
this is prelude for all of us to do.
A heart of gold is a spirit of pain.
My iron fist will show you that I care.

SONNET POEMS

WHAT IS PARADISE EXACTLY?

Paradise isn't always a mansion,
sometimes it means that you have peace of mind.
My independence is held for ransom,
as my freedom is in its tightest bind.

I'm livin' in tatters, yet I feel content,
where I don't need riches or approval.
I don't need the powers that's the consent,
as my being is not in upheaval.

I live for myself I don't need no one,
except to see life as it really is.
It may look pretty, but not always fun,
imperial gaze is a hit or miss.

Making one's paradise is up to you,
look inside at what you should always do.

WEAK FROM HEAD TO TOE

Getting tired with fatigue can break us,
as a deep sleep hypnotizes our will.
Out of nowhere comes heavy hypnosis,
drowsing our limbs and eyes enough to kill.

Wondering whether or not we may die,
we give into sleep and doze off in vain.
Should we pass on as soon as we all lie?
Depends how much our energy is drained.

Our eyes are heavier than most barbells,
as we scurry for the nearest bed for sleep.
While we know our desires all so well,
our time to live disintegrates far deep.

As we close our eyes and our limbs hold still,
we rest only to pass on unfulfilled.

TO SLEEP ONLY TO NEVER WAKE

If I fall asleep, I may never wake,
wondering where my resting place will be.
Could be in a bed, couch, hammock or lake,
as this heavy spell becomes much for me.

As I sleepwalk into my fluffy bed,
I dive head first into my comfort zone.
Without worry that I might be dead,
before I know, I may pass alone.

I must rebuild my strength nearing its end,
while resting may help me gain more power.
This may keep me alive free from harm and
help me sprout into that gorgeous flower.

Should I go drop dead when I go to sleep?
At least I'll die peacefully...so don't weep.

LOVE: GOOD FOR THE SOUL, BAD FOR THE MIND

Love is a terrible mental illness,
as it makes our mind race to confusion.
It makes us practice resilient stillness,
but gives us spiritual contusions.

Our hearts are hurting with great nervousness,
spotting that special someone we so love.
These feelings we endure bring great soreness,
just like God punishing us from above.

Maybe it's the devil's doing instead,
setting us up only, to knock us down.
Would God do this to us where this deep dread,
forces us to act with desperation?

Otherwise, this feeling's too much for me,
as it hurts me so bad that you can see.

CHAPELS OF THE BLEAK

Churches look a lot more like dark castles,
as they haunt us from the inside out.
These buildings give us such constant hassles,
knowing what we rebuke, the more we shout.

To love comes from our insides, not some lord,
who claims to love us, but won't let us live.
Human rights are our absolute reward,
it sounds like something that he just won't give.

I want to believe that he truly cares,
even though he bestows poor righteousness.
When I witness this scorn, I must beware,
the more that he loves us, I feel it less.

To believe what we want takes great courage,
to know when and why, is supreme knowledge.

THE DIFFERENCE BETWEEN GOOD AND EVIL

Is there a good or an evil on Earth?
On actions may or may not tell us that.
we may witness them as early as birth,
but the form of a dove or a black cat.

Even if we love, it still can be bad,
we can hate who we want and still be good.
The results of love can turn out so sad,
far worse than it is far worse than it should.

Sometimes I can't differentiate them,
as one's tonality throws me off course.
Their words can be astounding as gems,
but deceive me with brute and hurtful force.

I can't always decipher good and bad,
it brings an uncertainty never had.

LOVELORN, BUT NOT LOVED

If I love someone, but they don't love me,
are they still considered my first-time love?
There is a sight for the lovelorn to see,
as we wonder if, when push comes to shove.

The thrill of this scenario lives on,
remembering how this all made you feel.
Now wondering where these feeling have gone:
Why would this be considered a big deal?

What I'd give to have that feeling again,
to turn back the clock and relive that dream.
Sitting alone instead wondering when
I'll feel love hit me like a laser beam.

Thirsty to redeem this great adventure,
as I'm willing to handle this great venture.

ANSWERING TO THE HERD

In a world where we live on harsh judgment,
we pretend that it doesn't bother us.
This becomes a mind game and sad ailment,
which makes us all want to turn into dust.

The herd are a people that bring us down,
as they demand the world from everyone.
Even themselves, sink or swim, paddle or drown,
plug away until the job's fully done.

Otherwise you'll hear the roars in full force,
screamin' meanies, words of hate, hurtful tones.
It affects us all, but just stay the course,
words so bad to hear, they'll all break your bones.

Think that's scary, you ain't heard nothin' yet,
the crowd goes gun wild as the table's set.

FLOWERS

To escape the real world, look at flowers,
as they relax us deeply, unhappily.
Replenish us with unlimited powers,
give us gifts of strength we need constantly.

Even the most powerful need beauty,
as they dance with grace or lift heavy weights.
To remain happy or help the moody,
flowers bring us all smiles as it elates.

People get excited for baseball games,
barbeques, auto shows, a rock concert.
Other events in our world always reigns,
as we ignore beauty at our most curt.

In a life where emotion becomes king,
Serenity is what flowers can bring.

A MIND THAT SEGUES AT WARP SPEED

Lying in my room with some racing thoughts,
thinking away at rapid fire speed.
This behavior leaves my stomach in knots,
this isn't the stimulation I need.

With my mind travelin' around the world,
even while lyin' down, I just can't relax.
The frequent flier mileage that's been hurled,
my imagination's turned to the max.

From walking on air, to dancing in space,
from running through rough walls, living on the moon.
Exploring the universe place to place,
but somewhere, this adventure will end soon.

With a drop or two of melatonin,
that relaxation somewhere will set in.

PAY TO PLAY

I live in a world where I must not die,
as life is lived in ways which to survive.
We live only a short while, I can't lie,
so I do what I must go to thrive.

But even if I do, at least I lived,
where not many people really do that.
On some days alone, my life had drifted,
into strange people's houses I stayed at.

I paid to play, and boy, did I ever?
Most people pay a lot more for real love.
That's just too much for me, I could never
feel for one person that's more than enough.

Most people pretend to love and to give,
but do they ever pay to play...to live?

BLACK HOLE OF POP CULTURE

Hollywood's a black hole of pop culture,
people sell their souls for money and fame.
To live this life seems like an adventure,
win some, lose some, you gotta play the game.

Runnin' the gauntlet at each audition,
lookin' to score that part to change your life.
Method acting or impersonations,
this business will cut your throat with a knife.

Sex, drugs, rock 'n roll, megalomania,
are relics that make hollow souls look strong.
While the hacks cash in, it's hysteria
to see high-priced talent stifled too long.

It's not what you know, it's all who you know,
shit like this happens wherever you go.

JUNK FOOD ARE DRUGS

People get their high by eating like shit,
because the hole in their stomach's a void.
For every munch, by piece and bit,
it's the bad food that they need to avoid.

Burgers and Ho-Ho's are like crack cocaine,
one bite or sniff of them just ain't enough.
Pigging out's a habit that we all sustain,
through laziness 'cuz breakin' it's sure tough.

The best we can do is cure our cravings,
looking for answers that can heal us all.
We buy junk food that decrease our savings,
where our own finances can hit a wall.

Noshing and eating shit's like getting high,
too much of these things will cause us to die.

UNCHAINED

An unchained heart is someone that can't breathe,
it's like gagging someone's mouth shut from air.
This is suppression I just can't believe,
while others without this problem don't care.

With every attempt comes more struggles,
as hunger for air gets out of control.
Like a dog restricted with a muzzle,
only the heart can't function in its whole.

Being unable to bring life to me
scares me as I wonder so helplessly,
"How can I undergo, such a degree
of deprivation so relentlessly?"

This dream or exaggeration is deep,
makes me writhe in fear to my fatal sleep.

BODY AT EASE

I rest my body to remain alive,
as I sleep away in pure harmony.
My living room's a haven where I cry,
laugh, recline, and rest while watching TV.

My blood flows softly and sweetly inside,
me, weakened from the recliner's structure.
I kick up my legs as the chair provides
relaxation with a day of leisure.

I lay my head back and close my eyes shut,
only to empty my mind of rubbish.
As I sleep gracefully out of a rut,
that can leave me ragged more than sluggish.

It's okay to rest on a Saturday,
make sure you don't go limp and pass away.

BURNING HEARTS

Hearts of fire are a sign of passion,
when something burns inside and spreads around.
The heat gives you a growling obsession,
that desire turns you into a hound.

A hunger so big that makes you live strong,
gives you great immunity that will thrive.
There's a chance where the flame won't burn for long,
so we look down further to stay alive.

We search inside for ourselves, for meaning,
something within that passion we must use.
An intangible that's not so preening,
but something that gives us well needed clues.

As for what you want to do, you must choose,
for if you do but nothing, you will lose.

VENOM IN OUR VEINS

A disgusting venom lives in us all,
picking a way at our defanged feelings.
Awaiting the moment to find our gall,
to displace on those our inner feelings,

Where we try to rest that hidden demon,
that's when we burn to scream our loudest thought.
This gives us release that helps our breathin',
to help us win battles in which we've fought,

A tension rising makes us sick inside,
fiendin' to express rambunctious hunger.
With stillness and calm in which we confide,
we yearn to dwindle away our anger.

In this time of our great incubation,
we all police our own deep frustration.

SHAMES AND FLUKES

Worn out by a life's worth of shames and flukes,
one seems to wonder if it's worth living.
This is a hard life that not one rebukes,
but all despite a lifetime of giving,

from sharp hurts to bumpy and weary roads,
rich or poor...mostly poor, these adventures
embrace from cross country to our abode,
keep us wondering what's there to nurture.

Maybe it's time to credit our resolve,
as we live and greatly struggle in vain.
We look inside at what we need to solve,
since no one can help us wash off these stains.

That's the problem sometimes, we all need help,
but who cares to hear our loud, aching yelp?

DISHEARTENMENT AND ENCHANTMENT

It's one thing to have some disheartenment,
to feel empty...winded, rocked, dejected.
It's another to smile with enchantment,
and bring a strong front that I've injected.

Inside of me is a plague I don't want,
a nasty bottled up plague filled with great fear.
Though there is depth inside in which to haunt
others, I choose peace in how to appear.

Otherwise, I'm torn on how I should be,
with a fire burning holes in my gut.
While I wonder if the others can see,
soon enough, I feel like a mangy mutt.

With one errant word that may come my way,
this can turn into a mischievous day.

BATTLEFIELD OF HATE

My life is a battlefield of pure hate,
I have to fight to do what I want to.
This shouldn't be a grudge match or debate,
but I'm no pussy, I'm not gonna sue.

To even breathe is a constant battle,
to say what I feel has been restricted.
I must speak my truth, I just might tattle,
even if I'm chained up or convicted.

To burrow for a true self is to dig
a grave for one self. To take a chance.
That is to live without fear and go big,
with anything you have that will enhance.

We live our lives to sustain our being,
but we need vision to do our bidding.

MARATHON OF DOOM

Depression is a marathon of doom,
as I run it each day, dead to the world.
This is a testament of its great bloom,
from the negativity that I've hurled.

Just to put on my New Balance shoes suck,
as I have to dreadfully stretch myself.
Even if I finish, I still have bad luck,
running a race that still ruins my health.

Twenty-six miles of groans, moans, and big grunts,
where I still face the same problems again.
As dread and sadness remain on the hunt,
I'd rather be mauled in a lion's den.

No one likes to run unless it's from pain,
facing these ghouls flushes them down the drain.

LIVING OUR RAW THOUGHTS

Sometimes we do things we don't always mean,
our actions tell us what we really think.
We could be the worst people ever seen,
our behavior puts our trust on the brink.

As people begin to second guess us,
we question our motives so privately.
Our animal instincts make people cuss,
where they themselves behave so horribly.

It's hard to think before we do something,
believe it or not, it's hard to react.
Where people play citizens so soothing,
that they keep their own emotions intact.

Thinking or doing, our brain works so much,
to make rash decisions, to live as such.

BLINDED BY THE ARCTIC

In a setting so cold, my dreams are numb,
where I can't feel myself take in the wind.
I can't even see if the light will come,
as the sun is blocked while its cloud close in.

Its white gleaming atmosphere comes about,
with no view of where we all need to go.
Leaves us in a place of blindness and doubt,
wandering in a world we'll never know.

Everything is pitch white around us all,
where darkness is lighter than ever seen.
With sharp snowflakes on my cold face, I call,
"Help! I can't see!!!", as the snowfall gets mean.

Overall, it's not so bad to freeze deep,
into the arctic with a handy weep.

WAKING UP IS HARD TO DO

Waking up is hard to do all the time,
in the late night, it becomes much harder.
Getting out of bed's a mountain to climb,
drowsy and groggy, that's not what matters.

It's that you make sense of your surroundings,
when you're well rested, your mind's out of whack.
When you can't sleep your body of fuming,
all because you just couldn't sleep worth jack.

It's a conflicting problem that scorns us,
as our bad bodies drag through each hour.
With each day where we end up bitin' dust,
we become a nation feeling sour.

It's something that we have to do, it's sad,
waking up is hard to do...that's too bad!

STRIKE LIKE A RAM WITHOUT A DAMN

To feel a burning fire like I do,
it's unsettling, but it's necessary.
When something inside, feels like a big zoo
and I try to remain sedentary.

Still, I just want to be more destructive,
wait, more destructive? You don't see that way!
I have ways of making that conducive,
you're about to have a horrible day.

Don't think I'm unable to flip the switch,
because I need and want to fight, I will.
And when I do, your life will be a bitch,
as I'm one false move from ready to kill.

When that moon is full, I strike like a ram,
my flames spread recklessly, without a damn.

WHIRLWIND OF RAW EMOTION

I am a whirlwind of raw emotion,
shaped like a tornado, built like iron.
My tantrums have committed devotion,
no melatonin'll make me tired.

Meditation seems to be practical,
as it will help me relax and calm down.
But voicing displeasure is more tasteful,
even if it makes me look like a clown.

It's not fun to be angry all the time,
as losing my cool is quite the workout.
It burns me out at the drop of a dime,
but it's better to do so than to pout.

If we didn't have the feelings to vent,
our brilliance wouldn't make the world dent.

NEVER REST IN PEACE

I am a lingering insomniac,
where I can't bring myself to go to sleep.
Tension like this makes me a maniac,
and takes the concentration I can't keep.

Even if I shot myself, I'm still awake,
with a deep vigor that I never chose.
With my waning sanity now at stake,
my eyes as bloodshot red, may never close.

I only sleep when I don't feel like it,
but even if I do, I never will.
At an inopportune time I see fit,
I'll never be certain when to be still.

Death demands us to shut down completely,
though I'll never rest in peace contently.

TO CONTROL IS TO PROTECT

Sometimes I control myself when I can't,
but being controlled in general sucks.
Sometimes I'm controlled even when I rant,
we're all controlled so we can make big bucks.

But being told what to do ain't enough,
as we must embody your whole new self.
To live this way in our lives is so tough,
that we forget the true meaning of wealth.

It is to live without shame or regret,
which is a problem that most people have.
A matter of time before this begets
a lack of account that we all must have.

Control is a way to protect one self,
control is a way to retain our wealth.

LIFE

Life is a mind game that should never be,
A metaphysical and weary place.
Where we attempt to solve what we can't see,
It blows up in smoke and blinds our faces.

Life knocks us out when it just feels like it,
as we get back up when we don't want to.
Otherwise we will just keep getting hit,
hard enough not to get payback on you.

We face problems beyond our possession,
digging ourselves in and out of a hole.
Building and breaking our reputation,
causing growth to our hearts, minds, and our souls.

Life's an open road and a puzzling maze,
with problems for us to solve for each day.

ARNIE PYE IN THE SKY

Airplanes, helicopters, and Goodyear blimps,
zooming around the world into the sky,
Flown for our planet to catch a clear glimpse,
maybe someday I'll watch for Arnie Pye.

The famous Springfield traffic reporter
is like a great God looking down on us.
I wish I had my own tape recorder,
to hear his voice as he sounds like a wuss.

Otherwise, watching the aircrafts take flight
is a moment to reflect on one thing.
The plain or copter with our keen sight,
it's a wonder to watch something soothing,

So, sit on your roof or lay in the sand,
to watch the skies occupied, it's so grand.

TWO-FACED BEHEMOTH

Beauty is quite a mysterious thing,
it's not always what it may look to be.
You may never know what chaos it brings,
a two-faced behemoth for you and me.

Luscious and exquisite on the outside,
for all of us to drool and stare at it.
While underhanded and ruthless inside,
that can break our hearts and will quite a bit.

To love someone who wants your heart in chains,
is a careless decision one would make.
To await their response they won't refrain,
results in a world of endless heartbreak.

Ripping out your heart, it just before you die,
shows where their true intentions really lie.

POINT OF NO RETURN

The labor of love is a mystery,
as we all work for appreciation.
We have an end game for us all to see,
only to receive abomination.

As we care, cook, and clean, it's all for naught,
putting in elbow grease for that return.
Baking a cake, giving candy we bought,
only to suffer a heart wrenching burn.

With no one loving you back with passion,
it's the passion they use to hurt you with.
We all understand that blunt sensation,
with a scathing others see as a myth.

Most people happily endure those aches,
to learn to love more, whatever it takes.

CHASING A LIVING

Money is a bleak possession most want,
but it's a necessity all can't have.
Those who have it do all they can to taunt,
while the rest run for it, hurting their calves.

Chasing a living is never easy,
as for wasting money, this just ain't right.
To fund wars and to corrupt the sleazy,
where equal help for all is out of sight.

Facing financial peril frightens us,
and if it doesn't, it certainly should.
It inflates our anger that when we cuss,
inflation alone traps us when it could.

To go make us spend more than we want to,
plagues our living, no matter what we do.

THE NEIGHBORHOOD

Surrounded by blue skies and a dark shade,
it's a day that the sun won't skewer you.
It's more like a day to drink lemonade,
grill some hot dogs, burgers...even tofu.

Hearing the choppers chop and the airplanes fly,
while watching the stickball game in the street.
It's sheer excitement no one can deny,
with no mobile device, God what a treat!

With reckless cursing from the boys next door,
The flair, weather, and atmosphere possessed.
give the neighborhood bravado and more,
with one's adrenaline pumpin', no less.

Drama and attitude to stay afloat,
as urban moxie is something to gloat.

I CAN'T SLEEP BECAUSE I WON'T SLEEP

No matter how bad I want to stay down,
I continue to wake when I shouldn't.
When I open my eyes, I sport a frown,
as when it comes to sleep, I just couldn't.

I'm just too occupied to dream again,
as I hear the birds chirp at around three.
While I wake from my messy lion's den,
I wish that my demons would let me be.

Let me sleep 'till dawn or at least 'till ten,
with the radio playing 'SOU.
I just want figure out if and when,
I can sleep with nothing else left to do.

Even if I die before I can write,
I will rest in peace before the sunlight.

BIG GAME HUNTING

Love is a tough sport like big game hunting,
where guys want to make their mark on one girl.
With many lovely girls in the hunting,
this chauvinistic bullshit makes me hurl.

Showboating their way to desperation,
while the most humble, great men are just that.
Which is bad for their own disposition,
while the clueless, cocky ones go to bat.

There are so many good men that don't hunt,
as the look to stay true to decency.
The problem is that they may not be blunt,
to tell how they feel bombastically.

Enough games, men. Open your purest hearts,
let your deepest love jump right off the charts.

FREE VERSE POEMS

WHERE'S SAM?

I still think about
Sam sometimes,
Even though
she doesn't know
where I am.

She probably
doesn't want
to see me again
neither.

I stupidly wonder
where she is
even though she feels
safe after blocking me.

My heart isn't broken,
By my mind drifts
when I see her there
as I wonder
where she is and
who she's with.

Overall $15.00 per hour
may get me
a bigger bank account,
but no house or
apartment
any time soon.

BITTERNESS

Bitterness
is a poisonous
spell that I have
inside of me
where it hurts
to imagine
what could've been
if I said
"fuck you"
more often than not.

I feel regretful
for not being
rebellious in a piss poor pitiful
life I feel I relived.

My middle-aged years
are more care free,
but I need a surge,
something burning
that will make me
stand out as a
nobody who won't back down!

A BROKEN HEART ALWAYS BEATS

My heart
is the strongest
muscle
in my body
where it beats
just right after
it breaks into two.

How do muscles
break down though
when they can
only tear into pieces?

This is an unsolved mystery
that hurts me,
but only for a
little while,
as time heals this word
only to hurt
in private where
my mind races
while listening
to my
inner most thoughts.

WEATHER IS A MOOD

Today is mercurial
and has no true identity,
Changing moods of weather
several times today.

When I woke up, it was cloudy
when I went to work, it was sunny.
When I had lunch it was rainy,
but when I finished work, it was sunnier out.

Will it snow tonight
or will it hail?

Why can't I have one mood
for today?

Only human mood should change
from time to time,
Not weather because
I want to take in the sun.

Let it rain tomorrow
so I can write in the bar
and eat while reading
instead of scrolling aimlessly.

UNCERTAINTY IS A CERTAINTY

We are unsure about
a lot of things in this life.
Where I'm gonna work,
For how long, with who,
who I will love, hate,
and vice versa.

I'm even unsure
About the next line
or who is
in the audience
out to kill me.

All I know is that
I'm in a world where at face value,
Uncertainty is a certainty.

LIGHTS OUT

Sleep is like death,
but you're still breathing,
which means you can still
get up again and live
life while nodding off.

Tiredness becomes
a slower way of life
where you can only hope
to move as fast
as you are while
filled up with energy.

Once your eyes get heavy,
it's only a matter of time
until the eyelids break down
and the limbs run out of juice.

That's when you must choose
to either continue or call it a night.

Lights out.

WHERE'S THE LOVE?

I haven't loved much
due to not needing to,
but I wonder what
life would bring me.

I know I wouldn't be
nearly as happy
as I am right now
if I had boys and girls
rushing to see me
when I walk in the door
or a wife to cuddle with
at night to ease my blood flow.

Out of whack with a bad appetite
and tired because of it
because I noshed all day long
makes me lucky to go
straight upstairs to bed
without interruption.

EXPERIENCE THE HEAT

The heat is an
experience
that I can
never take in.
Even when I do,
it becomes a
weakening,
melting,
soul-sucking,
heart-wrench
that I don't
want to deal with.

I'm too tired
from all this
stickiness and
hot air that
I just want to
sit in front of an
air conditioner.

SOULFUL WORLD

A soulful world
has become more
open to us all.

While we express
our dismay and
discomfort,
there's a soulfulness
in that of itself.

To express one's self
in any way
possible
is to be soulful
in general.

WHO AM I?

Loneliness
is a world of
many acres,
but a bleak
population.

Imagine
being alone
on Earth
knowing that
most people don't
understand you.

It's just you
and your thoughts,
intuitions and
curiosities.

Who are you really
and who really cares?

While you're lonely,
Make sure you do
because no one else
ever will.

THE MYSTERY OF LIFE

I want to live,
but I don't know how
to want to live.

The mystery of life
is a crapshoot
within a crapshoot.

I need a
clear cut answer
why I'm here
on this earth.

Is my life more precious
than a mentally deficient
sixty-year-old man?

I feel as if
anyone's life
is different from
others based on
who you are.

Life's precious, sure,
just not yours.

THE AUTHOR OF REPRESSED RAGE

Heavy metal
is an author
of repressed rage,
which has yet to
have been unearthed.

We've seen all of the
bands of the past
bring the best out of
our disenfranchised public.

The world as a whole
needs a voice filled
with guttural power
and fury mixed with pain.

No matter what
instrument
you play or even
if your
body,
mind,
or soul

is one,
play it loud
that the deaf
can hear your
battle cry.

THE ILLUSION OF HAPPINESS

Happiness might be
an illusion where
we all wake up
feeling good.

Only to be surprised
about what the day
brings all of us,
we act on
adrenaline
and the allotted
time we have
on this day and
on this Earth.

Otherwise,
find something
in this maze
of a world
that gives you
a ray of joy
because outside
of it is another
life of hell.

GOLD: COLOR OF CHAMPIONS

Gold is a color
that people hold
to a high standard.

Most people don't
have an idea what
their favorite color
should really be.

They'll say that their
favorite color is
red, black, green, blue,
yellow, pink, brown, orange,
but you never here them
say that it's gold.

Every color you see
That people gravitate to,
believe it or not,
isn't gold,
but it should be.

Gold is the color
of a champion,
a winner, a true
gladiatorial
color of power.

It shines through
darkness while
glaring through
horror and brute
demonization
Gold is given
to those who
don't like the color,
but play to win.

STEAM OF FAILURES

I love the truth
of bitterness
because I can
unleash my wrath
and let off my steam
anyway, shape
and/or form.

Things go wrong
for everyone,
nothing is really
supposed to go
right for anyone.

For things to go well,
you need pure luck,
work hard, sacrifice,
go the extra mile,
yadda, yadda, yadda...

But when plans fall through
and you fail a lot,
you must express the
scorching fire that
the world turns you

into dust and blows you
into the air
where you travel
around the world
only to miss
the chance
to see the world,
but still
take in the
fresh air that
ushers you around
the globe back
into the ground.

THE CHORE OF TRUST

Slithering snakes
aren't exactly
what you see,
but what you
come in contact with.

At work,
in the streets,
at the bars,
drivin' you home
from the show,
whatever, whoever.

People sneak
around
to live the
life that they
always wanted
to bring a
versatility
that most people
never have.

They live in worlds
that you don't know about.

We live in worlds
that others don't know about.

The people you see
hide more than
you show them
and you shouldn't
show them
jackbone.

Trusting people
is a chore where
you have to watch
out for your feelings
while making sure
they protect theirs.

You're mirroring
each other while
trying to fuck
each other over.
Ain't love grand?

FORCE

Force is an attribute
that we have in which
we use to seize
our opportunities.

Some people have
a tenacity that
gives them the strength
to battle forces
bigger than them.

To test their might
In a world that has more,
but only with the
assistance of a
community combined.

Otherwise each and
Every person has
developed a force
through sacrifice
of the soul.

Force is a feeling,
a mood,
a tension,

a free spirit,
and a free flowing
phenomena.

We must embrace
our bull,
our ox,
our bison,
our black bear,
our raging animal.

Without force,
there is no
assurance of
a foundation of self.

SPIRIT OF METAL

Heavy metal
is a way of life
for us humans,
whether or not
we have
high or low
energy.

It is how to
use the energy
to take on a
life where
ups and downs
become a
way to live through
the tidal waves
that ebb and flow
us through the turmoil
that we are required
to live through,
whether we know
what comes or not.

Life is undefined,
but the spirit of
metal is in every
person to combat

each other for
whatever reason
to bring out the
greater good they
see that our
wretched planet
is in need for.

CLINGING ONTO LOVE

Clinging onto love
is a strong thing to do,
even though no one
loves you.

It's when you look
for love in wrong places
you're playing full on
Russian Roulette
with the people
who hate you worse
than you love them.

Love is pain when you
feel it in your heart
for someone who you love,
but doesn't love you back.

It's a double entendre
that batters the
heart and soul
until it sees that
you're sure to grow
into another
member of the lovelorn herd.

THE FARTHER AWAY, THE MORE BEAUTIFUL

The person you love
will be far more
beautiful than
you've ever imagined
when they're not
by your side.

Fuck them!

Absorb your losses
and channel your pain
into creation, but first
you must acknowledge
that pain or you'll
become oblivious to life
by seeing, but not knowing.

Wide eyes represent
blindness in the weirdest
way known to man,
while an intense look
sniffs out the worst
odors society can bring.

PAIN IS STRENGTH

Pain hurts, but still feels good
when you undergo a
throttling pain that
makes you want to cry.

You don't have to cry
if you don't want to
but don't be surprised
if you end up doing so.

Tears are unsettling
on our faces when they
come down rolling
like an avalanche of
hurt that comes and goes.

Expect yourself to cry
and embrace the death
you must have while living
a life of uncertainty
that can lead to doom
or handle the darkness.

JUST NOT IN THE CARDS

Not wanting to do
what you're supposed to
can get you in trouble,
but you just won't comply.

Will you?!?

Can you even comply
When you want to more
than anyone but can't?

As a circle that can't
fit in a square peg or
an orphan who can't
find a proper home,
it's hard for you because
no matter how willing
you are and you must be,
you will never be able
to achieve what you need
not what you want.
It's if they like you,
the light's on green.
If it's on red,
they'll stop you
before you start.

ANGER IS SUICIDE FOR ALL OF US

Anger is the worst thing
that we will have to deal with,
where it nullifies vulnerability
right before it heightens it
There's so much that can cause
someone to be upset over nothing
where they respond using great force.

Nobody likes to be angry,
nor do they like to
carry around a big bag
or shit in their diaphragm
where the tension of rage
is held for such a long period.

It's a heart attack
waiting to happen,
but even in the midst of an
epic temper tantrum,
you're about to keel over
anyway, no matter what.

SHIT IS AN OMNISCIENT CHAMELEON

Shit comes in all
shapes and sizes,
but we just have to
decide what to sweat
and what not to sweat.

There's so much of it
to go around that
you can't escape it,
whether you have
problems of your own
or people project
their problems onto you.

You can project your own shit
onto other people, but
your problems will
get worse as you won't
be able to make your
problems theirs, which will
cause you to become
even more upset.

Shit smells.
Shit is a mood.
Shit is a spirit animal.

MONEY IS THE #1 PROBLEM FOR US ALL

Money is the one thing
that ruins everything,
because people who
have it want more
and people who don't
have it need it, even
when people have
more money, they still
say that they need it
when they have too much
so they can find their
hobbies to make the
world a better place
when it's getting worse.

People need it to live
while the rich want
more of it to thrive
in a world where they
can diversify the Earth
to do more, but instead
diversify their portfolios.

If we didn't need money
to do anything,
things would be easier.

THE INNER TURMOIL SHOWCASE

I wish I didn't feel
as much as I do sometimes
because there's a price for
bearing your soul in the way
that your environment
becomes afraid of what
sit and watch you
self-destruct anyway...

Assholes!
Fuck it then!

Bare your soul and
ask for help, even
if you had to put on
a show to do it
free of admission.

A painful feeling that
we need to experience
is wanting to be heard
only for life to
shut us the fuck up.

That's when it's time
to explode at
a level so high
the other planets
will want to
recruit you to
destroy the
Earth.

THE MAIN EVENT

I wrestle with the
hate, love the sweet
and the sour that
lives inside of me.

Body slammin'
suplexin'
back breakin'
heart poundin'
good times
on the outside
that are bad times
on the inside
make me feel
like I'll be
wrestling each day
for as long as I live
and I don't always
need to so much.

My lifelong wrestling match
is against me each day
where I'm chest choppin'
the shit out of myself
to see what there is
to fix in order to be accepted
which killed me in the end.

While still alive,
believe it or not,
I'm still trying to kill
The innocence that I
Still have, but don't want.

As adults, we all fry to
weed out that child that
won't leave us so they
can grow up to be
the urban warlords that
we need to combat
the rich and then...
eat them.

CPSIA information can be obtained
at www.ICGtesting.com
Printed in the USA
BVHW041338090922
646647BV00013B/289/J